TOYS from Heaven

by Ruth L. Griffin

WestBow Press books may be ordered through booksellers or by contacting:

WestBow Press
A Division of Thomas Nelson & Zondervan
1663 Liberty Drive
Bloomington, IN 47403
www.westbowpress.com
844-714-3454

Scripture taken from the King James Version of the Bible.

ISBN: 978-1-6642-2425-4 (sc)
ISBN: 978-1-6642-2426-1 (e)

Library of Congress Control Number: 2021903365

Print information available on the last page.

WestBow Press rev. date: 04/05/2021

WESTBOW
PRESS®
A DIVISION OF THOMAS NELSON
& ZONDERVAN

Introduction

This book is based on Ephesians 4:8. "Wherefore he saith, when he ascended up on high, he led captivity captive and gave gifts unto men." The term "men" is translated from the Greek word anthrôpôs, a human being. Therefore, children are included in God's gift giving unto men. "Toys from Heaven" lovingly shows children the blessings of God's gifts. Reading and sharing this book with children will be exciting, enlightening and the Word will be sown into their hearts.

Dedication

This is book is dedicated to children all over the world.

In addition, I wrote "Journey To A Miracle" about my grand daughter Kayla. At 8 years old, God gifted her an amazing miracle. This book, "Toys from Heaven," connects the heart of a loving God to children.

Acknowledgements

First I thank God for giving me the inspiration to write what he wants for children to envision about Him. To God be all the glory and the praise!

To my daughter Denell, thank you for your technology and assistance in helping to get this book to the publisher. Thank you for your prayers and support. May God reward you abundantly!

To my grand daughter Kayla, thank you for your help in the designing of this book. May God give you your hearts desire!

To Apostle Epps, thank you for your prayers and encouragement! You have been a tremendous help. May God give you much favor!

To Keynia Hardley and Tricia Marshall, thank you for editing, I am truly grateful! Blessings!

It was Children's Day and there was a big celebration at my church. It was a very special day because it was also Miss Pauline's birthday. Miss Pauline was the Sunday School teacher for Joey, my seven-year old son. Joey had made a beautiful surprise birthday card for Miss Pauline.

He planned to give her the card after class. Joey was so happy he could hardly wait.

Joey was glad I was with him that Sunday. As soon as we arrived to Sunday school he ran directly to his class.

He sat with his classmates and I sat with the other parents. While I waited, I held the surprise birthday card in my hand. Joey was so proud of his card, so I did not want him to forget to give it to Miss Pauline.

In the meantime, Miss Pauline put on a show to teach the children why Christ died for them. To help her with the class program she used a teacher's helper named Miss Mary. At the beginning of the program, Miss Pauline gave Miss Mary clear instructions, "Don't send the toys down until I tell you."

Well, She had gotten so busy setting up the slide for all the toys to come down. She lined them up, and decided to test the slide. "Oops!" Miss Mary forgot what Miss Pauline had told her and sent one toy down. The toy went bouncing down the slide. Miss Pauline turned around and saw what happened. Miss Mary made a big mistake. Miss Mary quickly had to admit that she forgot and said, "I'm sorry!" They both were tickled and laughed.

Miss Pauline went on with her program. She showed the children how people were struggling. She told them that God sent his only Son down to earth. Miss Pauline told the children all about how God gave his life to help each of them.

She shared that Christ went back to his heavenly home and sent gifts for them. Then suddenly, before Miss Pauline could even get the words out of her mouth, it was happening: TOYS FROM HEAVEN! A sparkling gold and red toy train came down into the room. It was filled with toys.

There were toys of blue, green, red, and yellow like a rainbow. They were toys of all sizes and shapes, some large and small for the children. OH! The children were screaming and laughing with joy.

It was so exciting to see the children opening the beautiful toys from heaven with happy smiles on their faces. Each one had a beautiful gift.

Even Miss Pauline got a gift: a toy horse that was big enough for her to hug. She wrapped her arms around the horse and hugged him tight. Everyone got the biggest surprise of their life. I was so amazed by what was happening that I did not remember Joey's surprise birthday card for Miss Pauline. I looked down and the card was still in my hand.

Printed in the United States
by Baker & Taylor Publisher Services